HYMNS OF THE FAITHFUL SERIES

ADVENT
CHRISTMAS
EPIPHANY

WRITTEN BY
Richard Resch

Series editor: Thomas J. Doyle

This publication is available in braille and in large print for the visually impaired. Write to the Library for the Blind, 1333 S. Kirkwood Rd., St. Louis, MO 63122-7295; or call 1-800-433-3954.

All Scripture quotations are from the HOLY BIBLE, NEW INTERNATIONAL VERSION®. NIV®. Copyright © 1973, 1978, 1984 by International Bible Society. Used by permission of Zondervan Publishing House. All rights reserved.

The copyright for the hymns "From Heaven Above to Earth I Come" (pp. 15–16, 18–19) and "O Morning Star, How Fair and Bright" (pp. 23–24, 26–27) is administered by Augsburg Publishing House, Board of Publications of Lutheran Church in America, and Concordia Publishing House. Used by permission.

Copyright © 2000 Concordia Publishing House
3558 S. Jefferson Avenue, St. Louis, MO 63118-3968
Manufactured in the United States of America

All rights reserved. No part of this publication may be reproduced, stored in a retrieval system, or transmitted, in any form or by any means, electronic, mechanical, photocopying, recording, or otherwise, without the prior written permission of Concordia Publishing House.

1 2 3 4 5 6 7 8 9 10   09 08 07 06 05 04 03 02 01 00

Contents

HYMN 1
Comfort, Comfort These My People
Page 4

HYMN 2
Oh, Come, Oh, Come, Emmanuel
Page 7

HYMN 3
Savior of the Nations, Come
Page 12

HYMN 4
From Heaven Above to Earth I Come
Page 15

HYMN 5
Joy to the World
Page 20

HYMN 6
O Morning Star, How Fair and Bright
Page 23

Study Sheet 1

Comfort, Comfort These My People

Focus

1. Define *comfort*.

2. Describe a situation or event you encountered when you needed comfort. Who or what comforted you at this time?

3. Describe a situation or event when you comforted someone.

4. List as many situations or events you can think of when a person may need comfort. How are these events or situations similar?

Inform

Sing "Comfort, Comfort These My People" (LW 28).

1. *"Comfort, comfort these My people,*
   Speak of peace!" so says our God.
   "Comfort these who sit in darkness
   Groaning under sin's dread rod.
   To My people I proclaim
   Pardon now in Jesus' name.
   Tell them that their sins I cover,
   That their warfare now is over!"

2. *Yes, our sins the Lord will pardon,*
   Blotting out each dark misdeed.
   All that well deserved His anger
   He no more will see nor heed.
   We who languished many a day
   Under guilt now washed away,
   We exchange our pining sadness
   For His comfort, peace, and gladness!

3. *Now the herald's voice is crying*
   In the desert far and near,
   Calling us to true repentance,
   For the kingdom now is here!
   Oh, that warning cry obey,
   Oh, prepare for God a way,
   Let the valleys rise to meet Him,
   Let the hills bow down to greet Him!

4. *Straight must be what long was crooked;*
   Make the roughest places plain!
   Let your hearts be true and humble,
   Ready for His holy reign!
   Here the glory of the Lord
   Stands so graciously revealed
   That all people see the token
   That God's word is never broken!

1. Read Isaiah 40:1–8. What comfort does Isaiah prophesy to the people of Israel? List the "comforting" promises God makes to His people.

2. List the "comforting" promises made by God in the hymn stanzas.

HYMN ONE: Comfort, Comfort These My People

3. Compare the "comforting" promises made in Isaiah 40:1–8 to the hymn stanzas.

4. The text for the hymn was originally written to commemorate St. John the Baptist's Day. Why? See Matthew 3:1–12.

5. Why is this hymn appropriate for Advent—the time in which we prepare for the celebration of Christ's coming?

6. How has Jesus brought comfort to a sin-filled world? See Romans 5:6–12.

Connect

1. What situation(s) or event(s) have you recently faced for which you need comfort?

2. Read 2 Corinthians 1:3–7. How does Paul compare suffering to comfort? What might you say to St. Paul in response to these verses?

3. St. Paul suffered greatly throughout his life (see 2 Corinthians 11:23–29). After he recounts his suffering, what does Paul confess (see 2 Corinthians 12:9–10)? How is Jesus' grace sufficient to provide you comfort as you face weaknesses, insults, hardships, persecutions, and difficulties?

4. Reread Isaiah 40:8 and stanza 4 of the hymn. What promise is made in each? Why is it important for us to seek comfort in God's Word? See John 1:1, 14.

Vision

1. Spend time this week meditating on Isaiah 40:1–8; 2 Corinthians 1:3–7; 2 Corinthians 11:23–12:10; John 1:1–18; and "Comfort, Comfort These My People."

2. Share the comfort of God's Word with a friend or loved one who has faced hardships and difficulties.

3. Seek ways to bring comfort to the outcasts in your community. Visit a nursing home or convalescent center. Plan a Christmas celebration in which you invite some who will be alone on Christmas. Donate your time to provide assistance at a homeless shelter or help serve a meal to the hungry.

Study Sheet 2

Oh, Come, Oh, Come, Emmanuel

Focus

1. Have you ever eagerly awaited the arrival of a guest—a grandparent, brother or sister, cousin, or friend whom you had not seen in a very long time? You arranged the visit weeks or even months before the arrival. You thought about the visit every day in anxious anticipation. Sometimes it seemed that the day would never arrive. As the day of arrival drew closer, your excitement swelled until it seemed you just couldn't wait any longer. Describe a situation in which you experienced this type of anticipation.

2. The people of Israel had waited many years for the Messiah that God had promised. Compare the feelings the people of Israel had as they anticipated the arrival of this most honored guest to your feelings as you awaited the visit of your guest.

Inform

Sing together "Oh, Come, Oh, Come, Emmanuel" (*LW* 31).

1. *Oh, come, oh, come, Emmanuel,*
   And ransom captive Israel,
   That mourns in lonely exile here
   Until the Son of God appear.

   Refrain:
   Rejoice! Rejoice! Emmanuel
   Shall come to you, O Israel!

2. *Oh, come, our Wisdom from on high,*
   Who ordered all things mightily;
   To us the path of knowledge show,
   And teach us in her ways to go. Refrain

3. *Oh, come, oh, come, our Lord of might,*
   Who to Your tribes on Sinai's height
   In ancient times gave holy law,
   In cloud and majesty and awe. Refrain

4. *Oh, come, O Rod of Jesse's stem,*
   From ev'ry foe deliver them
   That trust Your mighty pow'r to save;
   Bring them in vict'ry through the grave. Refrain

5. *Oh, come, O Key of David, come,*
   And open wide our heav'nly home;
   Make safe the way that leads on high,
   And close the path to misery. Refrain

6. *Oh, come, our Dayspring from on high,*
   And cheer us by Your drawing nigh;
   Disperse the gloomy clouds of night,
   And death's dark shadows put to flight. Refrain

7. *Oh, come, Desire of nations, bind*
   In one the hearts of all mankind;
   Oh, bid our sad divisions cease,
   And be Yourself our King of Peace. Refrain

HYMN TWO: Oh, Come, Oh, Come, Emmanuel

1. The hymn includes a series of "O Antiphons." Historically, one of these antiphons was sung each day from December 17–23. Match the O Antiphon found in the hymnal to its scriptural reference.
   ___ *O Sapientia*—O Wisdom from on high
   ___ *O Adonai*—O Lord and leader of the house of Israel
   ___ *O Radix Jesse*—O Root of Jesse
   ___ *O Clavis David*—O Key of David
   ___ *O Oriens*—O Dayspring
   ___ *O Rex gentium*—O longed-for King
   ___ *O Emmanuel*—O Emmanuel

   A. Exodus 3:2–6; 6:6; 19–20
   B. Isaiah 11:1–11; Romans 15:11–12
   C. Ecclesiastes 1:2–3; Proverbs 24:3–7
   D. Genesis 49:10; Isaiah 7:14; 33:22; Matthew 1:23
   E. Revelation 3:7–8
   F. Psalm 24:7–10; Isaiah 32:1; Zechariah 9:9
   G. Malachi 4:2; Luke 1:79; John 8:12; Hebrews 1:3

2. How do the "O" statements describe the person and work of Emmanuel?

3. How does the hymn capture the emotion associated with the anticipated arrival of a guest?

4. How do we confess in the hymn that which has been fulfilled in the person and work of Jesus and that which will be completed on Judgment Day?

5. Why is it appropriate that each stanza of the hymn ends with the refrain: "Rejoice! Rejoice!"?

Connect

1. The Lord and Savior comes to us today in many ways. Describe the blessings and benefits you receive as the Lord comes to you in
   • His Word,
   • His Sacrament of Holy Baptism,
   • His Sacrament of the Lord's Supper.

2. How do we still today anticipate Jesus' Second Coming? What means does God provide us today to prepare for that visit?

3. Consider each of the "O" statements from the hymn. Which is most meaningful to you? Why?

4. How can every day of your life end with the refrain "Rejoice! Rejoice!"? How is this refrain appropriate even as you face death?

Vision

1. Meditate each day this week on one of the "O" statements and its scriptural reference.//
2. Begin and end your prayers each day during the following week by speaking or singing the refrain from the hymn.
3. Share with someone this week the meaning of Emmanuel—God with us—and how Emmanuel is the King of Peace in your life.

Oh, Come, Oh, Come, Emmanuel

Psalteriolum Cantionum Catholicarum, Köln, 1710
Tr. John M. Neale, 1818–66, alt.

VENI EMMANUEL
French processional, 15th cent.

1. Oh, come, oh, come, Emmanuel, And ransom captive Israel, That mourns in lonely exile here Until the Son of God appear.
2. Oh, come, our Wisdom from on high, Who ordered all things mightily; To us the path of knowledge show, And teach us in her ways to go.
3. Oh, come, oh, come, our Lord of might, Who to your tribes on Sinai's height In ancient times gave holy law, In cloud and majesty and awe.
4. Oh, come, O Rod of Jesse's stem, From ev'ry foe deliver them That trust your mighty pow'r to save; Bring them in vict'ry through the grave.

Setting copyright © 1982 Concordia Publishing House

5. Oh, come, O Key of David, come,
   And open wide our heav'nly home;
   Make safe the way that leads on high,
   And close the path to misery. *Refrain*

6. Oh, come, our Dayspring from on high,
   And cheer us by your drawing nigh;
   Disperse the gloomy clouds of night,
   And death's dark shadows put to flight. *Refrain*

7. Oh, come, Desire of nations, bind
   In one the hearts of all mankind;
   Oh, bid our sad divisions cease,
   And be yourself our King of Peace. *Refrain*

Study Sheet 3

Savior of the Nations, Come

Focus

1. "The Word became flesh and made His dwelling among us" (John 1:14). How would your life be different if God moved into your home?

2. The reality! Through faith in Jesus, God has made you His dwelling. As you contemplate this great truth, consider your hospitality to the one who lives in you.

3. If honest, we must confess that our lives have often not reflected a hospitality to God. We have rejected, betrayed, and ignored the one who made our lives His home. What is God's promise to us as we repent of these and all other sins? See 1 John 1:9.

Inform

Sing together "Savior of the Nations, Come" (*LW* 13).

1. *Savior of the nations, come,*
   Show Yourself the virgin's son.
   Marvel, heaven, wonder, earth,
   That our God chose such a birth.

2. *No man's pow'r of mind or blood*
   But the Spirit of our God
   Made the Word of God be flesh,
   Woman's offspring, pure and fresh.

3. *Here a maid was found with child,*
   Virgin pure and undefiled.
   In her virtues it was known
   God had made her heart His throne.

4. *Then stepped forth the Lord of all*
   From His pure and kingly hall;
   God of God, becoming man,
   His heroic course began.

5. *God the Father was His source,*
   Back to God He ran His course.
   Into hell His road went down,
   Back then to His throne and crown.

6. *Father's equal, You will win*
   Vict'ries for us over sin.
   Might eternal, make us whole;
   Heal our ills of flesh and soul.

7. *From the manger newborn light*
   Sends a glory through the night.
   Night cannot this light subdue,
   Faith keeps springing ever new.

8. *Glory to the Father sing,*
   Glory to the Son, our king,
   Glory to the Spirit be
   Now and through eternity.

HYMN THREE: *Savior of the Nations, Come*

1. Although the stanzas are short, each one provides "rich theological food." What theological truth is found in each stanza?

2. The reality of Christ is at times dimmed by an almost storybook treatment of Christmas. What evidence can you provide from this hymn that "Savior of the Nations, Come" paints the picture of the *real* state of humanity and the *real* meaning of God's intervention in the world?

3. How does the hymn emphasize the reality of John 1:14?

4. Why do you think this hymn, associated with the First Sunday in Advent, is also a favorite for Christmas Eve and Christmas Day celebrations?

Connect

1. How might you use "Savior of the Nations, Come" as a tool in responding to someone who asks, "What is the true meaning of Christmas?"

2. Describe the significance of John 1:14 for your life. Consider stanza 6 of the hymn.

3. How effectively does the hymn illustrate the reality of people's sin? God's intervention for people in the person and work of Jesus? Give reasons for your answers.

Vision

1. Today begin meditating on each stanza of the hymn and the significance of the message of each stanza for your life.

2. Share the real meaning of Christmas with a friend or loved one using "Savior of the Nations, Come."

3. Consider new ways that you and your congregation can make the truth of this hymn reality for people of all nations.

Savior of the Nations, Come

Attr. St. Ambrose, 340–97
German version, Martin Luther, 1483–1546
Tr. F. Samuel Janzow, b. 1913, alt.

NUN KOMM, DER HEIDEN HEILAND
Johann Walter, *Geystliche gesangk Buchleyn,* 1524

1. Savior of the nations, come,
   Show yourself the virgin's son.
   Marvel, heaven, wonder, earth,
   That our God chose such a birth.

2. No man's pow'r of mind or blood
   But the Spirit of our God
   Made the Word of God be flesh,
   Woman's offspring, pure and fresh.

3. Here a maid was found with child,
   Virgin pure and undefiled.
   In her virtues God of God,
   Being it was known God had made her heart his throne.

4. Then stepped forth the Lord of all
   From his pure and kingly hall;
   God of God, becoming man,
   His heroic course began.

5. God the Father was his source,
   Back to God he ran his course.
   Into hell his road went down,
   Back then to his throne and crown.

6. Father's equal, you will win
   Vict'ries for us over sin.
   Might eternal, make us whole;
   Heal our ills of flesh and soul.

7. From the manger newborn light
   Sends a glory through the night.
   Night cannot this light subdue,
   Faith keeps springing ever new.

8. Glory to the Father sing,
   Glory to the Son, our king,
   Glory to the Spirit be
   Now and through eternity.

Text copyright © 1978 Concordia Publishing House
Setting copyright © 1982 Concordia Publishing House

Study Sheet 4
From Heaven Above to Earth I Come

Focus

1. What images first come to mind when you think of the Christmas story?

2. For many of us the images of Mary, Joseph, the baby Jesus, the innkeeper, the angels, and the shepherds were first planted in our minds and fixed in our memory by the yearly enactment of the Christmas story in a worship service. Today, some congregations go to great efforts to reenact the story of Jesus' birth not only for members and visitors to a worship service, but also for the community in a "living manger scene" performed out of doors. What is the benefit of reenacting yearly the story of Jesus' birth?

Inform

Sing together "From Heaven Above to Earth I Come" (LW 37–38).

1. From heav'n above to earth I come
   To bring good news to ev'ryone!
   Glad tidings of great joy I bring
   To all the world and gladly sing:

2. To you this night is born a child
   Of Mary, chosen virgin mild;
   This newborn child of lowly birth
   Shall be the joy of all the earth.

3. This is the Christ, God's Son most high,
   Who hears your sad and bitter cry;
   He will Himself your Savior be
   And from all sin will set you free.

4. The blessing which the Father planned
   The Son holds in His infant hand
   That in His kingdom, bright and fair,
   You may with us His glory share.

5. These are the signs which you will see
   To let you know that it is He:
   In manger bed, in swaddling clothes
   The child who all the earth upholds.

6. How glad we'll be to find it so!
   Then with the shepherds let us go
   To see what God for us has done
   In sending us His own dear Son.

7. Look, look, dear friends, look over there!
   What lies within that manger bare?
   Who is that lovely little one?
   The baby Jesus, God's dear Son.

8. Welcome to earth, O noble Guest,
   Through whom this sinful world is blest!
   You turned not from our needs away!
   How can our thanks such love repay?

9. O Lord, You have created all!
How did You come to be so small
To sweetly sleep in manger bed
Where lowing cattle lately fed?

10. Were earth a thousand times as fair
And set with gold and jewels rare,
Still such a cradle would not do
To rock a prince so great as You.

11. For velvets soft and silken stuff
You have but hay and straw so rough
On which as king so rich and great
To be enthroned in humble state.

12. O dearest Jesus, holy child,
Prepare a bed, soft, undefiled,
A holy shrine, within my heart,
That You and I need never part.

13. My heart for very joy now leaps;
My voice no longer silence keeps;
I too must join the angel throng
To sing with joy His cradlesong:

14. "Glory to God in highest heav'n,
Who unto us His Son has giv'n."
With angels sing in pious mirth:
A glad new year to all the earth!

1. Compare Luke 2:1–20 to "From Heaven Above to Earth I Come."

2. Martin Luther wrote this hymn for his family's celebrations of Christmas. Stanzas 1–5 were sung by a family member dressed as an angel. Stanzas 7–14 were sung by the individual children as a response to the angel's message. Stanza 6 was sung by the entire family. What benefits do you think Luther's children received from the Christmas Eve activity?

3. Luther wrote in the margin of this hymn that it was to be used in all future hymnals and with the children. Why do you suppose Luther believed this hymn was so important?

4. *Lutheran Worship* designated the first seven stanzas as "Part 1—The Angel's Message" and the remaining stanzas as "Part 2—Our Response." Is this an appropriate designation? Why?

Connect

1. How might this hymn be used in your home to celebrate Christmas?

2. This hymn is a ballad—it tells a story. Describe in your own words the story it tells and the importance of the story for your life.

3. Why is it important that children experience Jesus' birth in song, in story, and in reenactment from an early age?

Vision

1. Use this hymn in family devotions to review and to rehearse the story of Jesus' birth.

2. Illustrate the stanzas of the hymn with your family. Use crayons, colored pencils, markers, or paints.

3. Tell someone this week the significance of Jesus coming from heaven above to earth.

4. Consider how you can provide opportunities to fix the images of the Christmas narrative in the minds and hearts of your children and/or your children's children.

From Heaven Above to Earth I Come

Martin Luther, 1483–1546　　　　　　　　　　　　　　　　VOM HIMMEL HOCH
Tr. *Lutheran Book of Worship,* 1978　　　　　Valentin Schumann, *Geistliche Lieder,* 1539

1. From heav'n above to earth I come To bring good news to ev-'ry-one! Glad tid-ings of great joy I bring To all the world and glad-ly sing:
2. To you this night is born a child Of Mar-y, cho-sen vir-gin mild; This new-born child of low-ly birth Shall be the joy of all the earth.
3. This is the Christ, God's Son most high, Who hears your sad and bit-ter cry; He will him-self your Sav-ior be And from all sin will set you free.
4. The bless-ing which the Fa-ther planned The Son holds in his in-fant hand That in his king-dom, bright and fair, You may with us his glo-ry share.

5. These are the signs which you will see
   To let you know that it is he:
   In manger bed, in swaddling clothes
   The child who all the earth upholds.

6. How glad we'll be to find it so!
   Then with the shepherds let us go
   To see what God for us has done
   In sending us his own dear Son.

Text copyright © 1978 *Lutheran Book of Worship*
Setting copyright © 1982 Concordia Publishing House

7. Look, look, dear friends, look over there!
   What lies within that manger bare?
   Who is that lovely little one?
   The baby Jesus, God's dear Son.

8. Welcome to earth, O noble Guest,
   Through whom this sinful world is blest!
   You turned not from our needs away!
   How can our thanks such love repay?

9. O Lord, You have created all!
   How did You come to be so small
   To sweetly sleep in manger bed
   Where lowing cattle lately fed?

10. Were earth a thousand times as fair
    And set with gold and jewels rare,
    Still such a cradle would not do
    To rock a prince so great as You.

11. For velvets soft and silken stuff
    You have but hay and straw so rough
    On which as king so rich and great
    To be enthroned in humble state.

12. O dearest Jesus, holy child,
    Prepare a bed, soft, undefiled,
    A holy shrine, within my heart,
    That You and I need never part.

13. My heart for very joy now leaps;
    My voice no longer silence keeps;
    I too must join the angel throng
    To sing with joy His cradlesong:

14. "Glory to God in highest heav'n,
    Who unto us His Son has giv'n."
    With angels sing in pious mirth:
    A glad new year to all the earth!

Study Sheet 5
Joy to the World

Focus

1. What is your favorite Christmas hymn or Christmas carol? Why?

2. Invariably, when asked this question, someone from a group will choose "Joy to the World." Why do you think this hymn is such a favorite?

Inform

Sing together "Joy to the World" (*LW* 53).

1. *Joy to the world, the Lord is come!*
   Let earth receive its King;
   Let ev'ry heart prepare Him room
   And heav'n and nature sing,
   And heav'n and nature sing,
   And heav'n, and heav'n and nature sing.

2. *Joy to the earth, the Savior reigns!*
   Let all their songs employ
   While fields and floods,
   rocks, hills, and plains
   Repeat the sounding joy,
   Repeat the sounding joy,
   Repeat, repeat the sounding joy.

3. *No more let sin and sorrow grow*
   Nor thorns infest the ground;
   He comes to make His blessings flow
   Far as the curse is found,
   Far as the curse is found,
   Far as, far as the curse is found.

4. *He rules the world*
   with truth and grace
   And makes the nations prove
   The glories of His righteousness
   And wonders of His love,
   And wonders of His love,
   And wonders, wonders of His love.

1. Read Psalm 98. How does "Joy to the World" reflect the truth revealed in the psalm through words and music?

2. "Joy to the World" is a significant expression of Christmas to the world. How is this a great blessing to the Christian church as it fulfills that which Jesus commanded in Acts 1:8? How is this a great blessing to those who are not Christians?

3. Describe how this hymn reveals the Law—our need for a Savior because of sin—and the Gospel—God's intervention on our behalf in the person and work of Jesus to forgive our sins?

Connect

1. What are your earliest recollections of the hymn "Joy to the World"?

2. How does this hymn express God's work on your behalf and your response to that work?

3. How is "Joy to the World" a confession of faith, hope, and joy *of* believers and *to* unbelievers?

4. Make a list of your favorite Christmas hymns or carols. Then explain the reason each is your favorite.

5. Sing some of your study group's favorite Christmas hymns or carols.

Vision

1. When you hear "Joy to the World" playing in the mall, on the street, or in the grocery store this Christmas season, make a point to tell someone why it means so much to you.

2. Meditate on the words of Psalm 98 this week.

3. Begin and end each day during the coming week singing or speaking the words to "Joy to the World."

Study Sheet 6

O Morning Star, How Fair and Bright

Focus

1. Open any newspaper or watch any newscast and you will find evidence of the darkness of sin in this world. What recent events demonstrate this darkness?

2. As Christians we often witness the effects of this darkness in our lives and the lives of others. When have you experienced this darkness?

3. Although darkness surrounds us, we, through faith, live in the light—the Light of the World—Jesus Christ. He conquered sin, death, and the power of the devil through His death on the cross and proclaimed victory for us over darkness when He rose from the dead. What difference does this truth mean for your life—even as you encounter darkness in your life?

Inform

Sing together "O Morning Star, How Fair and Bright" (LW 73).

1. O Morning Star, how fair and bright!
   You shine with God's own truth and light,
     Aglow with grace and mercy!
   Of Jacob's race, King David's son,
   Our Lord and master, You have won
     Our hearts to serve You only!
   Lowly, holy!
   Great and glorious,
   All victorious,
   Rich in blessing!
   Rule and might o'er all possessing!

2. Come, heav'nly bridegroom, light divine,
   And deep within our hearts now shine;
     There light a flame undying!
   In Your one body let us be
   As living branches of a tree,
     Your life our lives supplying.
   Now, though daily
   Earth's deep sadness
   May perplex us
   And distress us,
   Yet with heav'nly joy You bless us.

HYMN SIX: O Morning Star, How Fair and Bright

3. Lord, when You look on us in love,
    At once there falls from God above
        A ray of purest pleasure.
    Your Word and Spirit, flesh and blood
    Refresh our souls with heav'nly food.
        You are our dearest treasure!
    Let Your mercy
    Warm and cheer us!
    Oh, draw near us!
    For You teach us
    God's own love through You has reached us.

4. Almighty Father, in Your Son
    You loved us when not yet begun
        Was this old earth's foundation!
    Your Son has ransomed us in love
    To live in Him here and above:
        This is Your great salvation.
    Alleluia!
    Christ the living,
    To us giving
    Life forever,
    Keeps us yours and fails us never!

5. What joy to know, when life is past,
    The Lord we love is first and last,
        The end and the beginning!
    He will one day, oh, glorious grace,
    Transport us to that happy place
        Beyond all tears and sinning!
    Amen! Amen!
    Come, Lord Jesus!
    Crown of gladness!
    We are yearning
    For the day of Your returning.

6. Oh, let the harps break forth in sound!
    Our joy be all with music crowned,
        Our voices gaily blending!
    For Christ goes with us all the way—
    Today, tomorrow, ev'ry day!
        His love is never ending!
    Sing out! Ring out!
    Jubilation!
    Exultation!
    Tell the story!
    Great is He, the King of glory!

1. How does the truth of "O Morning Star, How Fair and Bright" reflect that which is proclaimed in Psalm 45?

2. Read Revelation 22:12–16. What comfort do these words provide? Which stanzas of the hymn reflect the truths in Revelation 22:12–16?

3. The text of this hymn, written by Philipp Nicolai, was first published in 1599 in response to the devastation of the plague upon the citizens of Unna in Westphalia. What evidence of assurance and comfort do the words of this hymn provide for Christians even as they face incredible sadness and trials?

4. What truth do Christians confess in this hymn?

5. Although this hymn is usually associated with the liturgical season of Epiphany, it was so popular in Germany that its lines and verses were written on earthenware, and it was sung and played at weddings and certain festivals. Why do you think the hymn enjoyed this incredible popularity?

Connect

1. Reread the stanzas of the hymn. Select your favorite and tell why it is your favorite.

2. On what occasion(s) might you consider using this hymn?

3. How might you use this hymn to tell others the reason for your joy in the midst of troubles and hardships?

Vision

1. As you encounter darkness in this world, pull out the words to this hymn and meditate on the Light of the World.

2. Tell a friend or loved one the reason for your joy even in the midst of sadness, sorrow, and hardships.

3. Reread Psalm 45 and Revelation 22:12–16 in your personal devotions this week.

O Morning Star, How Fair and Bright

Philipp Nicolai, 1556–1608
Tr. *Lutheran Book of Worship*, 1978

WIE SCHÖN LEUCHTET
Philipp Nicolai, 1556–1608

1. O Morning Star, how fair and bright! You shine with God's own truth and light, Aglow with grace and mercy! Of Jacob's race, King David's son, Our Lord and master, you have won Our hearts to serve you only!

2. Come, heav'nly bridegroom, light divine, And deep within our hearts now shine; There light a flame undying! In your one body let us be As living branches of a tree, Your life our lives supplying.

3. Lord, when you look on us in love, At once there falls from God above A ray of purest pleasure. Your Word and Spirit, flesh and blood, Refresh our souls with heav'nly food. You are our dearest treasure!

4. Almighty Father, in your Son You loved us when not yet begun Was this old earth's foundation! Your Son has ransomed us in love To live in him here and above: This is your great salvation.

Text copyright © 1978 *Lutheran Book of Worship*

5. What joy to know, when life is past,
   The Lord we love is first and last,
      The end and the beginning!
   He will one day, oh, glorious grace,
   Transport us to that happy place
      Beyond all tears and sinning!
   Amen! Amen!
   Come, Lord Jesus!
   Crown of gladness!
   We are yearning
   For the day of your returning.

6. Oh, let the harps break forth in sound!
   Our joy be all with music crowned,
      Our voices gaily blending!
   For Christ goes with us all the way—
   Today, tomorrow, ev'ry day!
      His love is never ending!
   Sing out! Ring out!
   Jubilation!
   Exultation!
   Tell the story!
   Great is he, the King of glory!